THE
ESSENTIAL
WISDOM
OF THE
FOUNDING
FATHERS

THE
ESSENTIAL
WISDOM
OF THE
FOUNDING
FATHERS

EDITED BY
CAROL KELLY-GANGI

FALL RIVER PRESS

New York

To John with love.

FALL RIVER PRESS

New York

An Imprint of Sterling Publishing Co., Inc.
1166 Avenue of the Americas
New York, NY 10036

ISBN 978-1-4351-6853-4

Distributed in Canada by Sterling Publishing Co., Inc.
c/o Canadian Manda Group, 664 Annette Street
Toronto, Ontario M6S 2C8, Canada
Distributed in the United Kingdom by GMC Distribution Services
Castle Place, 166 High Street, Lewes, East Sussex BN7 1XU, England
Distributed in Australia by NewSouth Books
45 Beach Street, Coogee, NSW 2034, Australia

For information about custom editions, special sales, and premium
and corporate purchases, please contact Sterling Special Sales at
800-805-5489 or specialsales@sterlingpublishing.com.

Manufactured in the United States of America

2 4 6 8 10 9 7 5 3 1

sterlingpublishing.com

Cover design by David Ter-Avanesyan
Interior design by Bruce McKillip

CONTENTS

✳ ✳ ✳ ✳ ✳

INTRODUCTION

✳   ✳   ✳   ✳   ✳

Ever since the founding of the American republic, the country has split along deep political divides. Today is no different. It seems that each day brings a new issue that spurs passionate discourse about the core values and fundamental ideals at the heart of the American identity. Amid the turmoil, it can be useful to revisit the words of the Founding Fathers for a measure of inspiration, fortitude, and guidance.

The Essential Wisdom of the Founding Fathers gathers hundreds of quotations from the leaders and patriots who conceived of and created the American experiment, thereby forging a new republic that has endured for more than 240 years.

Of course, the giants of American history such as George Washington, John Adams, Benjamin Franklin, Alexander Hamilton, Thomas Jefferson, James Madison, and Thomas Paine are richly represented in these pages. But the lesser-known Founding Fathers each played a singular role in the fledgling nation's struggle for independence; their work is included here as well.

In the selections that follow, George Washington implores his troops to keep fighting for the cause of liberty; Thomas Paine rails against the tyranny to which the colonists have been subjected; Thomas Jefferson and Alexander Hamilton each warn of the dangers of limiting the free press; James Madison cautions against the gradual encroachments on freedom; John Jay expounds on the dictates of justice; and John Adams extols the value of checks and balances for the three branches of government.

Elsewhere, the Founders exchange their passionate views on the supremacy of law and the equal protection it affords; the meaning of patriotism; the necessity of virtue; the art of diplomacy; the pitfalls of politics; and the role of religion. Still other excerpts reveal a more personal side of the patriots: John Adams and Thomas Jefferson long for the comforts of home and family; George Washington ponders the nature of true friendship; Benjamin Franklin wistfully recalls his beloved son Franky and the pride he feels for his grandson Benny; and Thomas Jefferson and Henry Lee reveal their great reverence for George Washington.

The Essential Wisdom of the Founding Fathers invites readers to view America through the eyes of the men who fought mightily to defeat an empire and create the first modern democracy, and who devoted their lives to the ideals that remain an integral part of the American landscape.

—CAROL KELLY-GANGI
2018

THE REVOLUTIONARY WAR

Then join hand in hand, brave Americans all! By uniting we stand, by dividing we fall!

—**John Dickinson**, *"The Liberty Song,"* 1768

This is the most magnificent movement of all! There is a dignity, a majesty, a sublimity, in this last effort of the patriots that I greatly admire. The people should never rise without doing something to be remembered—something notable and striking. This destruction of the tea is so bold, so daring, so firm, intrepid and inflexible, and it must have so important consequences, and so lasting, that I can't but consider it as an epocha in history!

—**John Adams**, *diary entry on the Boston Tea Party*, DECEMBER 17, 1773

The die is cast. The people have passed the river and cut away the bridge.

—**John Adams**, *writing about the Boston Tea Party*, DECEMBER 1773

Blandishments will not fascinate us, nor will threats of a "halter" intimidate. For, under God, we are determined that wheresoever, whensoever, or howsoever we shall be called to make our exit, we will die free men.

—**Josiah Quincy III**, *responding to the closing of Boston Harbor by the British*, 1774

A settled plan to deprive the people of all the benefits, blessings, and ends of the contract, to subvert the fundamentals of the constitution, to deprive them of all share in making and executing laws, will justify a revolution.

—**John Adams**, Novanglus Papers, 1774

The God who gave us life, gave us liberty at the same time.

—**Thomas Jefferson**, Summary View of the Rights of British America, 1774

We live, my dear soul, in an age of trial.

What will be the consequences,

I know not.

—John Adams, *letter to*
Abigail Adams, 1774

Sink or swim, live or die, survive or perish, I am with my country from this day on. You may depend on it.

—**John Adams**, *letter to a friend*, 1774

I am not a Virginian, but an American.

—**Patrick Henry**, *speech from the First Continental Congress*, OCTOBER 14, 1774

I am often concerned for you and our dear babes, surrounded, as you are, by people who are too timorous and too much susceptible of alarms. Many fears and jealousies and imaginary dangers will be suggested to you, but I hope you will not be impressed by them. In case of real danger, of which you cannot fail to have previous intimations, fly to the woods with our children.

—**John Adams**, *letter to Abigail Adams*, MAY 2, 1774

Don't tread on me!

—*Motto on first American flag, raised by* **John Paul Jones** *on the flagship* Alfred, DECEMBER 3, 1775

There is no retreat but in submission and slavery. Our chains are forged. Their clanking may be heard on the plains of Boston. The war is inevitable. And let it come! I repeat it, sir, let it come! It is in vain, sir, to extenuate the matter. Gentlemen may cry, peace, peace—but there is no peace. The war is actually begun. The next gale that surveys from the north will bring to our ears the clash of resounding arms. Our brethren are already in the field! Why stand idle here? Is life so dark or peace so sweet as to be purchased at the price of chains—and slavery? Forbid it, Almighty God! I know not what course others may take; but as for me, give me liberty or give me death!

—**Patrick Henry,** *speaking to the Virginia legislature,* MARCH 23, 1775

Colonel Washington appears at Congress in his uniform, and, by his great experience and abilities in military matters, is of much service to us. O that I were a soldier! I will be. I am reading military books. Everybody must, and I will, and shall, be a soldier.

—**John Adams,** *letter to Abigail Adams,* MAY 29, 1775

In the language of the Holy Writ, there is a time for all things. There is a time to preach and a time to fight. And now is the time to fight.

—**John Peter Gabriel Muhlenberg,** *speaking to his congregation in 1775 before leaving to join General Washington's troops in Virginia*

I beg it may be remembered by every gentleman in the room that
I this day declare, with the utmost sincerity, I do not think myself
equal to the command I am honored with. As to pay, sir, I beg leave
to assure the Congress that no pecuniary consideration could have
tempted me to accept this arduous employment at the expense of my
domestic ease and happiness, I do not wish to make any profit from it.

—**George Washington**, *accepting*
position as commander in chief of the
Continental Army, JUNE 1775

What a glorious morning is this.

—**Samuel Adams**, *on hearing gunfire*
at Lexington, APRIL 19, 1775

You may believe me, my dear Patsy, when I assure you in the
most solemn manner, that, so far from seeking this appointment,
I have used every endeavor in my power to avoid it not only from
my unwillingness to part from you and the family but from a
consciousness of its being a trust too great for my capacity, and that
I should find more real happiness in one month with you at home,
than I have the most distant prospect of finding abroad, if my stay
were to be seven times seven years. But as it has been a kind of
destiny, that has thrown me upon this service, I shall hope that my
undertaking it is designed to answer some good purpose.

—**George Washington**, *on heading*
the Continental Army, letter to
Martha Washington, JUNE 1775

As Britain began to use force, it seemed absolutely necessary that we should be prepared to repel force with force. It is a true old saying that make yourself sheep and the wolves will eat you: to which I may add another, God helps them that help themselves. The General was secure, I suppose, that we would never be able to return the outrage in kind; but the defeat of a great body of his troops by the country people at Lexington, and the action at Bunker's Hill, in which they were twice repulsed, and the third time gained a dear victory, was enough to convince the ministers that the Americans can fight, and that this was a harder nut to crack than they imagined.

—**Benjamin Franklin,** *from his autobiography*

Stand your ground. Don't fire unless fired upon. But if they mean to have a war let it begin here!

—**John Parker,** *captain of American forces, to his troops prior to the Battle of Lexington,* APRIL 19, 1775

I can answer for but three things: a firm belief in the justice of our cause, close attention in the prosecution of it, and the strictest integrity.

—**George Washington,** *letter to Colonel Burwell Bassett,* JUNE 19, 1775

Don't one of you fire 'til you see the whites of their eyes.

—**William Prescott,** *colonel of American forces, to his troops before the Battle of Bunker Hill,* JUNE 17, 1775

The reflection upon my situation and that of this army produces many an uneasy hour when all around me are wrapped in sleep. Few people know the predicament we are in.

—**George Washington**, *letter to Joseph Reed*, JANUARY 14, 1776

There is something very unnatural and odious in a government a thousand leagues off. A whole government of our own choice, managed by persons whom we love, revere, and can confide in, has charms in it for which men will fight.

—**John Adams**, *letter to Abigail Adams*, MAY 17, 1776

I am well aware of the toil and blood and treasure that it will cost to maintain this Declaration, and support and defend these States. Yet through all the gloom I can see the rays of ravishing light and glory. I can see that the end is worth more than the means.

—**John Adams**, *letter to Abigail Adams*, JULY 3, 1776

Every post is honorable in which a man can serve his country.

—**George Washington**, *letter to Benedict Arnold*, SEPTEMBER 14, 1775

Before God, I believe the hour has come. My judgement approves this measure, and my whole heart is in it. All that I have, and all that I am, and all that I hope in this life, I am now ready here to stake upon it. And I leave off as I began, that live or die, survive or perish, I am for the Declaration. It is my living sentiment, and by the blessing of God it shall be my dying sentiment. Independence now, and Independence for ever!

—**John Adams**, *speaking at the Continental Congress to the delegates from the Thirteen Colonies*, JULY 1, 1776

What has commonly been called rebellion has more often been nothing but a manly and glorious struggle in opposition to the lawless power of rebellious kings and princes. If ye love wealth better than liberty, the tranquility of servitude better than the animating contest of freedom, go home from us in peace. We ask not your counsels or arms. Crouch down and lick the hands which feed you. May your chains set lightly upon you, and may posterity forget that ye were our countrymen.

—**Samuel Adams**, *speech at State House in Philadelphia*, AUGUST 1, 1776

The time is now near at hand which must probably determine whether Americans are to be freemen or slaves; whether they are to have any property they can call their own; whether their houses and farms are to be pillaged and destroyed, and themselves consigned to a state of wretchedness from which no human efforts will deliver them. The fate of unborn millions will now depend, under God, on the courage and conduct of this army. Our cruel and unrelenting enemy leaves us only the choice of brave resistance, or the most abject submission. We have, therefore, to resolve to conquer or die.

—**George Washington,** *address to the
Continental Army before the battle of
Long Island,* AUGUST 27, 1776

The period of debate is closed. Arms, as the last resource, decide the contest. . . . The blood of the slain, the weeping voice of nature cries, 'Tis time to part.

—**Thomas Paine,** Common Sense, 1776

I only regret that I have but one life to lose for my country.

—**Nathan Hale**

Let us therefore animate and encourage each other, and show the whole world that a Freeman, contending for liberty on his own ground, is superior to any slavish mercenary on earth.

—**George Washington**, *general orders from his headquarters, New York,* JULY 2, 1776

Victory or Death.

—**George Washington** *wrote this inscription on a scrap of paper while speaking to Benjamin Rush about the desperate state of his army just days before leading them across the frozen Delaware River in a surprise attack on Hessian troops at the Battle of Trenton on* DECEMBER 26, 1776

These are the times that try men's souls. The summer soldier and the sunshine patriot will, in this crisis, shrink from the service of their country; but he that stands it now, deserves the love and thanks of man and woman. Tyranny, like hell, is not easily conquered; yet we have this consolation with us, that the harder the conflict, the more glorious the triumph.

—**Thomas Paine**, The American Crisis, No. 1, DECEMBER 19, 1776. *Washington ordered his commanders to read the essay to their men on* DECEMBER 25, 1776, *prior to crossing the Delaware River for the Battle of Trenton*

You have done all I asked you to do, and more than could be reasonably expected. But your country is at stake, your wives, your homes and all that you hold dear. You have worn yourselves out with fatigues and hardships, but we know not how to spare you. If you will consent to stay only one month longer, you will render that service to the cause of liberty and to your country which you probably never can do under any other circumstance.

—**George Washington,** *imploring his troops to reenlist,* DECEMBER 30, 1776

We fight not to enslave, but to set a country free, and to make room upon the earth for honest men to live in.

—**Thomas Paine,** The American Crisis, No. 4, SEPTEMBER 12, 1777

As to the history of the revolution, my ideas may be peculiar, perhaps singular. What do we mean by the revolution? The war? That was no part of the revolution; it was only an effect and consequence of it. The revolution was in the minds of the people, and this was effected from 1760 to 1775, in the course of fifteen years, before a drop of blood was shed at Lexington.

—**John Adams,** *letter to Thomas Jefferson,* AUGUST 24, 1815

No history, now extant, can furnish an instance of an army's suffering such uncommon hardships as ours has done, and bearing them with the same patience and fortitude. To see men without clothes to cover their nakedness, without blankets to lie on, without shoes, by which their marches might be traced by the blood from their feet . . . and submitting to it without a murmur, is a mark of patience and obedience which in my opinion can scarce be paralleled.

—**George Washington**, *letter written from Valley Forge to John Banister,* APRIL 21, 1778

It having pleased the Almighty Ruler of the universe to defend the cause of the United American States, and finally to raise up a powerful friend among the princes of the earth, to establish our liberty and independence upon a lasting foundation, it becomes us to set apart a day for gratefully acknowledging the divine goodness, and celebrating the important event, which we owe to His divine interposition.

—**George Washington**, *order issued from Valley Forge in response to the news that France had entered the war on the side of the Colonies,* MAY 5, 1778

The citizens of America . . . are, from this period, to be considered as the actors on a most conspicuous theater, which seems to be peculiarly designated by Providence for the display of human greatness and felicity.

—**George Washington**, Circular to the States, 1783

We must, indeed, all hang together or, most assuredly, we shall all hang separately.

—Benjamin Franklin, *at the signing of the Declaration of Independence, JULY 4, 1776*

In news from America, I received a large and particular account of Gen. Benedict Arnold's plot. . . . He tried to draw others after him, but in vain; not a man followed him. Judas sold only one man, Arnold three millions; Judas got for his one man 30 pieces of silver, Arnold not a halfpenny a head. A miserable bargainer, especially when one considers the quantity of infamy he acquir'd to himself and entail'd on his family. I found his baseness and treachery astonishing! He was despised even by those who expected to be serv'd by his treachery. His character was, in the sight of all Europe, already on the gibbet, and will hang there in chains for ages.

—**Benjamin Franklin**, *from his autobiography*

I have not yet begun to fight.

—**John Paul Jones**, *commander of the* Bonhomme Richard *(Poor Richard), responding to a British commander on* SEPTEMBER 23, 1779, *who yelled from his ship asking if Jones was ready to surrender after Jones's ship was nearly destroyed. The British convoy surrendered after three hours of fighting.*

Our hopes are not placed in any particular city or spot of ground, but in preserving a good army, furnished with proper necessaries, to take advantage of favorable opportunities, and waste and defeat the enemy by piecemeal.

—**Alexander Hamilton**, *letter to Hugh Knox,* 1777

Glorious news! The Duke de Lauzun arrived at Versailles from
Virginia with the happy news of the combined force of America
and France having forced General Cornwallis to capitulate. . . .
It is a rare circumstance, and scarce to be met with in history, that
in one war an army should have been taken prisoners completely
and not a man escaping. It is another singular circumstance that an
expedition so complex, form'd of armies of different nations and of
land and sea forces, should with such perfect concord be assembled
from different places by land and water, and form their junction
punctually, without the least being retarded by cross accidents of
wind or weather, or interruption from the enemy. . . . No expedition
was ever better plann'd or better executed. It made a great addition
to the military reputation Gen. Washington had already acquired,
and brightened the glory that surrounds his name and that must
accompany it to our latest posterity.

> —**Benjamin Franklin**, *from his autobiography,*
> *reacting to the news of Cornwallis's surrender in*
> OCTOBER 1781 *after the Battle at Yorktown. The*
> *peace treaty with England to officially end the war*
> *would not be fully negotiated and signed until* 1783.

THE FOUNDING OF
THE NATION

Yesterday, the greatest question was decided which ever was debated in America, and a greater perhaps never was nor will be decided among men. A resolution was passed without one dissenting colony, "that these United Colonies are, and of right ought to be, free and independent States."

—**John Adams**, *letter to Abigail Adams,*
JULY 3, 1776

We hold these truths to be self-evident, that all men are created equal, that they are endowed by their creator with certain unalienable rights, that among these are life, liberty, and the pursuit of happiness.

—**Thomas Jefferson**, *The Declaration of Independence*, JULY 4, 1776

The second day of July 1776, will be the most memorable epoch in the history of America. I am apt to believe that it will be celebrated by succeeding generations as the great anniversary festival. It ought to be commemorated as the day of deliverance, by solemn acts of devotion to God Almighty. It ought to be solemnized with pomp and parade, with shows, games, sports, guns, bells, bonfires, and illuminations, from one end of this continent to the other, from this time forward forevermore.

—**John Adams,** *second letter to*
Abigail Adams, JULY 3, 1776

Reason first: You are a Virginian and a Virginian ought to appear at the head of this business. Reason second: I am obnoxious, suspected and unpopular. You are very much otherwise. Reason third: You can write ten times better than I can.

—**John Adams to Thomas Jefferson,** *on*
why the latter was the better choice to draft
the Declaration of Independence, 1776

Do you recollect the pensive and awful silence which pervaded the house when we were called up, one after another, to the table of the President of Congress to subscribe what was believed by many at that time to be our own death warrants?

—**Benjamin Rush,** *letter to John Adams,* 1781

When I signed the Declaration of Independence I had in view not only our independence from England but the toleration of all sects.

—**Charles Carroll**, *letter to G. W. Parke Custis*, FEBRUARY 20, 1829

Driven from every other corner of the earth, Freedom of Thought and The Right of Private Judgment in matters of conscience direct their course to this happy country as their last asylum.

—**Samuel Adams**, *speech at State House in Philadelphia*, AUGUST 1, 1776

The said states hereby severally enter into a firm league of friendship with each other, for their common defence, the security of their Liberties, and their mutual and general welfare.

—**Articles of Confederation**, NOVEMBER 15, 1777

Resolved, that the flag of the thirteen United States be thirteen stripes, alternate red and white, that the Union be thirteen stars, white in a blue field, representing a new constellation.

—**Continental Congress**, 1777

In the name of the Most Holy and Undivided Trinity. It having pleased the Divine Providence to dispose the hearts of the most serene and potent Prince George the Third, by the Grace of God, King of Great Britain, France, and Ireland, Defender of the Faith. . . . and of the United States of America, to forget all past misunderstandings and differences.

—**Peace Treaty between the United States and Great Britain,** *Congress of the Confederation,* 1783

We the people of the United States, in order to form a more perfect union, establish justice, insure domestic tranquility, provide for the common defense, promote the general welfare, and secure the blessings of liberty to ourselves and our posterity, do ordain and establish this Constitution for the United States of America.

—**Preamble to the Constitution,** SEPTEMBER 17, 1787

I have often . . . in the course of the session . . . looked at that sun behind the President without being able to tell whether it was rising or setting. But now at length I have the happiness to know it is a rising and not a setting sun.

—**Benjamin Franklin,** *on the final day of the Constitutional Convention,* SEPTEMBER 1787

I like the dreams of the future better than the
history of the past.

I have lived, Sir, a long time, and the longer I live, the more convincing proofs I see of this truth—that God Governs the affairs of men. And if a sparrow cannot fall to the ground without His notice, is it probable that an empire can rise without His aid?

—**Benjamin Franklin**, *Constitutional Convention*, SEPTEMBER 1787

I wish the Constitution which is offered, had been made more perfect; but I sincerely believe it is the best that could be obtained at this time—and, as a constitutional door is opened for amendment hereafter—the adoption of it, under the present circumstances of the Union, is in my opinion desirable.

—**George Washington**, *letter to Patrick Henry*, SEPTEMBER 24, 1787

It seems to have been reserved to the people of this country, by their conduct and example, to decide the important question, whether societies of men are really capable or not of establishing good government from reflection and choice, or whether they are forever destined to depend for their political constitutions on accident and force.

—**Alexander Hamilton**, The Federalist Papers, No. 1, OCTOBER 27, 1787

They accomplished a revolution which has no parallel in the annals of human society. They reared the fabrics of governments which have no model on the face of the globe. They formed the design of a great Confederacy, which it is incumbent on their successors to improve and perpetuate.

> —**James Madison,** The Federalist Papers,
> No. 14, NOVEMBER 30, 1787

This constitution . . . squints toward monarchy, and does not this raise indignation in the breast of every true American?

> —**Patrick Henry,** *expressing his opposition*
> *to the Constitution and the notion of*
> *a strong central government,* 1788

Our new Constitution is now established, and has an appearance that promises permanency; but in this world nothing can be said to be certain, except death and taxes.

> —**Benjamin Franklin,** *letter to Jean*
> *Baptiste Le Roy,* NOVEMBER 13, 1789

The Constitution is a mere thing of wax in the hands of the judiciary, which they may twist and shape into any form they please.

> —**Thomas Jefferson,** *letter to Judge*
> *Spencer Roane,* SEPTEMBER 6, 1819

Our Constitution was made only for a moral and religious people. It is wholly inadequate to the government of any other.

—**John Adams** *to the Officers of the
First Brigade of the Third Division of the
Massachusetts Militia,* OCTOBER II, 1798

I wish the bald eagle had not been chosen as the representative of our country; he is a bird of bad moral character; like those among men who live by sharping and robbing, he is generally poor, and often very lousy. The turkey is a much more respectable bird, and withal a true original native of America.

—**Benjamin Franklin,** *letter to
Sarah Bache,* JANUARY 26, 1784

It is part of the American character to consider nothing as desperate, to surmount every difficulty by resolution and contrivance.

—**Thomas Jefferson,** *letter to Martha
Jefferson Randolph,* MARCH 28, 1787

If there be one principle more deeply rooted than any other in the mind of every American, it is that we should have nothing to do with conquest.

—**Thomas Jefferson,** *letter to
William Short,* JULY 28, 1791

It is our true policy to steer clear of permanent alliances with any portion of the foreign world.

—George Washington, *Farewell Address*, SEPTEMBER 17, 1796

This country and this people seem to have been made for each other.

—John Jay, The Federalist Papers, No. 2, OCTOBER 31, 1787

I always consider the settlement of America with reverence and wonder, as the opening of a grand scene and design in Providence for the illumination of the ignorant, and the emancipation of the slavish part of mankind all over the earth.

—John Adams, *notes for* A Dissertation on the Canon and the Feudal Law, FEBRUARY 1765

It will be worthy of a free, enlightened, and, at no distant period, a great nation, to give to mankind the magnanimous and too novel example of a People always guided by an exalted justice and benevolence.

—George Washington, *Farewell Address*, SEPTEMBER 17, 1796

America, an immense territory, favour'd by nature with all advantages of climate, soil, great navigable rivers and lakes, &c., was destined to become a great country, populous and mighty; and would in a less time than was generally conceive'd be able to shake off any shackles that might be impos'd on her, and perhaps place them on the imposters.

—**Benjamin Franklin,** *from his autobiography*

GOVERNMENT
AND DEMOCRACY

What is government itself but the greatest of all reflections on human nature? If men were angels, no government would be necessary. If angels were to govern men, neither external nor internal controls on government would be necessary.

—**James Madison**, The Federalist Papers,
No. 51, FEBRUARY 6, 1788

A popular government without popular information, or the means of acquiring it, is but a prologue to a farce or a tragedy; or, perhaps both. Knowledge will forever govern ignorance. And a people who mean to be their own governors must arm themselves with the power which knowledge gives.

—**James Madison**, *letter to
W. T. Barry*, AUGUST 4, 1822

Why has government been instituted at all? Because the passions of men will not conform to the dictates of reason and justice without constraint.

Society in every state is a blessing, but government even in its best state, is but a necessary evil; in its worst state, an intolerable one.

—**Thomas Paine**, Common Sense, 1776

If the government is in the hands of a few, they will tyrannize the many; if in the hands of the many, they will tyrannize over the few.

—**Alexander Hamilton**, *letter to Robert Morris*, APRIL 30, 1781

As the happiness of the people is the sole end of government, so the consent of the people is the only foundation of it, in reason, morality, and the natural fitness of things.

—**John Adams**, *proclamation adopted by the Council of Massachusetts Bay*, 1774

The whole art of government consists in the art of being honest.

—**Thomas Jefferson**, from Works, VI, 1786

A government of laws, and not of men.

—**John Adams**, Novanglus Papers, 1774

Governments are instituted among men, deriving their just powers from the consent of the governed.

—**Thomas Jefferson,** *Declaration of Independence,* JULY 4, 1776

Metaphysicians and politicians may dispute forever, but they will never find any other moral principle or foundation of rule or obedience, than the consent of governors and governed.

—**John Adams,** Novanglus Papers, 1774

The government is the strongest of which every man feels himself a part.

—**Thomas Jefferson,** *letter to H. D. Tiffin,* FEBRUARY 2, 1807

There is no kind of dishonesty into which otherwise good people more easily and frequently fall than that of defrauding the government.

—**Benjamin Franklin,** *from his autobiography*

The spirit of resistance to government is so valuable on certain occasions that I wish it to be always kept alive. It will often be exercised when wrong, but better so than not to be exercised at all.

—**Thomas Jefferson**, *letter to Abigail Adams*, FEBRUARY 2, 1787

There is danger from all men. The only maxim of a free government ought to be to trust no man living with power to endanger the public liberty.

—**John Adams**, *notes for an oration at Braintree, Massachusetts*, 1772

I am not among those who fear the people. They, and not the rich, are our dependence for continued freedom.

—**Thomas Jefferson**, *letter to Samuel Kercheval*, JULY 12, 1816

I know no safe depository of the ultimate powers of society but the people themselves; and if we think them not enlightened enough to exercise their control with a wholesome discretion, the remedy is not to take it from them, but to inform their discretion by education.

—**Thomas Jefferson**, *letter to W. C. Jarvis*, SEPTEMBER 28, 1820

Among [European governments], under pretense of governing, they have divided their nations into two classes, wolves and sheep.

—**Thomas Jefferson,** *letter to Edward Carrington,* JANUARY 16, 1787

It always has been, and will continue to be, my earnest desire to learn and to comply, as far as is consistent, with the public sentiment; but it is on great occasions only, and after time has been given for cool and deliberate reflection, that the real voice of the people can be known.

—**George Washington,** *letter to Edward Carrington,* MAY 1, 1796

The execution of the laws is more important than the making of them.

—**Thomas Jefferson,** *letter to the Abbé Arnoux,* JULY 19, 1789

Happy it is when the interest which the government has in the preservation of its own power, coincides with a proper distribution of the public burdens, and tends to guard the least wealthy part of the community from oppression!

—**Alexander Hamilton,** The Federalist Papers, No. 36, JANUARY 8, 1788

A wise and frugal Government, which shall restrain men from injuring one another, shall leave them otherwise free to regulate their own pursuits of industry and improvement, and shall not take from the mouth of labor the bread it has earned. This is the sum of good government.

—**Thomas Jefferson**, *First Inaugural Address*, MARCH 4, 1801

Agriculture, manufactures, commerce, and navigation, the four pillars of our prosperity, are the most thriving when left to individual enterprise.

—**Thomas Jefferson**, *First Annual Message to Congress*, DECEMBER 8, 1801

Great confusion about the words democracy, aristocracy, monarchy. . . . Democracy in my sense, where the whole power of the government in the people, whether exercised by themselves or by representatives, chosen by them either mediately or immediately and legally accountable to them. . . . Consequence, the proposed government a representative democracy. . . . Constitution revocable and alterable by the people. This representative democracy as far as is consistent with its genius has all the features of good government.

—**Alexander Hamilton**, *on the Constitution*, 1788

When annual elections end, there slavery begins.

—**John Adams**, Thoughts on Government, 1776

Democratical States must always feel before they can see: it is this that makes their Governments slow, but the people will be right at last.

—**George Washington**, *letter to Marquis de Lafayette*, JULY 25, 1785

It has been observed that a pure democracy, if it were practicable, would be the most perfect government. Experience has proved that no position is more false than this. The ancient democracies, in which the people themselves deliberated, never possessed one feature of good government. Their very character was tyranny; their figure deformity.

—**Alexander Hamilton**, *speech to Congress*, JUNE 21, 1788

The preservation of the sacred fire of liberty and the destiny of the republican model of government are justly considered, perhaps, as deeply, as finally staked on the experiment entrusted to the hands of the American people.

—**George Washington**, *First Inaugural Address*, APRIL 30, 1789

The very idea of the power and the right
of the People to ·establish Government
presupposes the duty of every Individual to
obey the established Government.

—George Washington, *Farewell Address*, SEPTEMBER 17, 1796

The republican is the only form of government which is not eternally at open or secret war with the rights of mankind.

—**Thomas Jefferson,** *letter to William Hunter,* 1790

Some men look at Constitutions with sanctimonious reverence and deem them like the Ark of the Covenant—too sacred to be touched.

—**Thomas Jefferson,** *letter to Samuel Kercheval,* JULY 12, 1816

The liberty of the press consists in the right to publish with impunity truth with good motives, for justifiable ends. To disallow it is fatal.

—**Alexander Hamilton,** Propositions on the Law of Libel, 1804

I will now tell you what I do not like. First, the omission of a bill of rights, providing clearly, and without the aid of sophism, for freedom of religion, freedom of the press, protection against standing armies, restriction of monopolies, the eternal and unremitting force of the habeas corpus laws, and trials by jury, in all matters of fact triable by the law of the land, and not by the laws of nations.

—**Thomas Jefferson,** *letter to James Madison,* 1787

I have a right to nothing which another has a right to take away. And Congress will have a right to take away trial by jury in all civil cases. Let me add that a bill of rights is what the people are entitled to against every government on earth, general or particular, and what no just government should refuse or rest on inference.

—**Thomas Jefferson**, *letter to*
James Madison, 1787

Congress shall make no law respecting an establishment of religion, or prohibiting the free exercise thereof; or abridging the freedom of speech, or of the press; or the right of the people peaceably to assemble, and to petition the government for a redress of grievances.

—**The First Amendment**, *ratified*
as part of The Bill of Rights, 1791

Be not intimidated, therefore, by any terrors, from publishing with the utmost freedom whatever can be warranted by the laws of our country; nor suffer yourselves to be wheedled out of your liberty by any pretenses of politeness, delicacy, or decency. These, as they are often used, are but three different names for hypocrisy, chicanery, and cowardice.

—**John Adams**, A Dissertation on the Canon
and the Feudal Law, 1765

I am for . . . freedom of the press and against all violations of the Constitution to silence by force, and not by reason, the complaints or criticisms, just or unjust, of our citizens against the conduct of their agents.

—**Thomas Jefferson**, *letter to
Elbridge Gerry*, JANUARY 26, 1799

Subject opinion to coercion: whom will you make your inquisitors? Fallible men; men governed by bad passions, by private as well as public reasons. And why subject it to coercion? To produce uniformity. But is uniformity of opinion desirable? No more than of face and stature.

—**Thomas Jefferson**, Virginia Act for
Religious Freedom, 1786

History I believe furnishes no example of a priest-ridden people maintaining a free civil government. This marks the lowest grade of ignorance, of which their political as well as religious leaders will always avail themselves for their own purpose.

—**Thomas Jefferson**, *letter to
Baron von Humboldt*, 1813

To the press alone, chequered as it is with abuses, the world is indebted for all the triumphs which have been gained by reason and humanity over error and oppression. . . .

—**James Madison**, *Report on the Virginia and Kentucky Resolutions*, 1799

I will not condescend to employ the word Toleration. I assert that unlimited freedom of religion, consistent with morals and property, is essential to the progress of society and the amelioration of the condition of mankind.

—**John Adams**, *letter to Francis van der Kemp*, OCTOBER 2, 1818

I must admit, moreover, that it may not be easy, in every possible case, to trace the line of separation, between the rights of Religion & the Civil authority, with such distinctness, as to avoid collisions & doubts on unessential points. The tendency to a usurpation on one side, or the other, or to a corrupting coalition or alliance between them, will be best guarded against by an entire abstinence of the Government from interference, in any way whatever, beyond the necessity of preserving public order, & protecting each sect against trespasses on its legal rights by others.

—**James Madison**, *letter to Jasper Adams*, SEPTEMBER 1833

THE PRESIDENCY

I walk on untrodden ground. There is scarcely any action, whose motives may not be subject to a double interpretation. There is scarcely any part of my conduct which may not hereafter be drawn into precedent.

—**George Washington**, *letter to Catharine Sawbridge Macaulay Graham*, JANUARY 9, 1790

His character was, in its mass, perfect, in nothing bad, in few points indifferent; and it may truly be said that never did nature and fortune combine more perfectly to make a man great.

—**Thomas Jefferson** *on George Washington, letter to Dr. Walter Jones*, JANUARY 2, 1814

Had I been chosen president again, I am certain I could not have lived another year.

—John Adams, *from his autobiography*

For myself the delay [in assuming the office of the president] may be compared with a reprieve; for in confidence I assure you, with the world it would obtain little credit that my movements to the chair of Government will be accompanied by feelings not unlike those of a culprit who is going to the place of his execution: so unwilling am I, in the evening of a life nearly consumed in public cares, to quit a peaceful abode for an Ocean of difficulties, without that competency of political skill, abilities and inclination which is necessary to manage the helm.

—**George Washington**, *comment to Henry Knox*, MARCH 1789

To the memory of the Man, first in war, first in peace, and first in the hearts of his countrymen.

—**Henry Lee III**, *from his eulogy of George Washington*, DECEMBER 1799

Whether I should say, "Mr. Washington," "Mr. President," "Sir," "may it please your Excellency," or what else? I observed that it had been common while he commanded the army to call him "His Excellency," but I was free to own it would appear to me better to give him no title but "Sir" or "Mr. President," than to put him on a level with a governor of Bermuda.

—**John Adams**, *seeking advice of the Senate for a title for President George Washington*, 1789

All see, and most admire, the glare which hovers round the external trappings of elevated office. To me there is nothing in it, beyond the lustre which may be reflected from its connection with a power of promoting human felicity.

—**George Washington**, *letter to Catharine
Sawbridge Macaulay Graham*, JANUARY 9, 1790

The only question that labors in my mind is, whether I shall retire with [President Washington]. I hate to live in Philadelphia in summer, and I hate still more to relinquish my farm. I hate speeches, messages, addresses and answers, proclamations, and such affected, studied, constrained things. I hate levees and drawingrooms. I hate to speak to a thousand people to whom I have nothing to say. Yet all this I can do.

—**John Adams**, *March* 1, 1796

Among the vicissitudes incident to life no event could have filled me with greater anxieties than that of which the notification was transmitted by your order. . . . The magnitude and difficulty of the trust to which the voice of my country called me, being sufficient to awaken in the wisest and most experienced of her citizens a distrustful scrutiny into his qualifications, could not but overwhelm with despondence one, who, inheriting inferior endowments from nature and unpracticed in the duties of civil administration, ought to be peculiarly conscious of his own deficiencies.

—**George Washington**, *First
Inaugural Address*, APRIL 30, 1789

The situation in which I now stand, for the last time, in the midst of the Representatives of the People of the United States, naturally recalls the period when the Administration of the present form of Government commenced; and I cannot omit the occasion, to congratulate you and my Country, on the success of the experiment; nor to repeat my fervent supplications to the Supreme Ruler of the Universe, and Sovereign Arbiter of Nations, that his Providential care may still be extended to the United States; that the virtue and happiness of the People, may be preserved; and that the Government, which they have instituted, for the protection of their liberties, may be perpetual.

—**George Washington,** *Eighth Annual Address to Congress,* DECEMBER 7, 1796

He seemed to enjoy a triumph over me. Methought I heard him say, "Ay! I am fairly out and you fairly in! See which of us will be happiest!"

—**John Adams,** *the day after his inauguration, on George Washington's congratulations to him at the inauguration,* MARCH 4, 1797

I have no ambition to govern men. It is a painful and thankless office.

—**Thomas Jefferson,** *letter to John Adams,* DECEMBER 28, 1796

I know well that no man will ever bring out of that office the reputation which carries him into it. The honeymoon would be as short in that case as in any other, and its moments of ecstasy would be ransomed by years of torment and hatred.

—**Thomas Jefferson**, *letter to Edward Rutledge*, DECEMBER 27, 1796

Called upon to undertake the duties of the first executive office of our country, I avail myself of the presence of that portion of my fellow citizens which is here assembled, to express my grateful thanks for the favor with which they have been pleased to look toward me, to declare a sincere consciousness that the task is above my talents, and that I approach it with those anxious and awful presentiments which the greatness of the charge and the weakness of my powers so justly inspire.

—**Thomas Jefferson**, *First Inaugural Address*, MARCH 4, 1801

The second office of the government is honorable and easy, the first is but a splendid misery.

—**Thomas Jefferson**, *letter to Elbridge Gerry*, MAY 13, 1797

An executive is less dangerous to the liberties of the people when in office during life, than for seven years.

—**Alexander Hamilton,** *speaking at the Constitutional Convention,* JUNE 18, 1787

No man who ever held the office of President would congratulate a friend on obtaining it. He will make one man ungrateful, and a hundred men his enemies, for every office he can bestow.

—**John Adams,** *upon the election of his son,*
John Quincy Adams, to the presidency, 1824

The danger is that the indulgence and attachments of the people will keep a man in the chair after he becomes a dotard. . . . General Washington set the example of voluntary retirement after eight years. I shall follow it. And a few more precedents will oppose the obstacle of habit to any one after awhile who shall endeavor to extend his term.

—**Thomas Jefferson,** *letter to*
John Taylor, JANUARY 6, 1805

You are afraid of the one—I, of the few. We agree perfectly that the many should have a full, fair and perfect Representation.—You are Apprehensive of Monarchy; I, of Aristocracy. I would therefore have given more Power to the President and less to the Senate.

—**John Adams,** *letter to Thomas*
Jefferson, DECEMBER 6, 1787

FREEDOM AND RIGHTS

I would define liberty to be a power to do as we would be done by.
The definition of liberty to be the power of doing whatever the law
permits, meaning the civil laws, does not seem satisfactory.

—**John Adams,** *letter to J. H.*
Tiffany, MARCH 31, 1819

The tree of liberty must be refreshed from time to time with the
blood of patriots and tyrants. It is its natural manure.

—**Thomas Jefferson,** *letter to Colonel*
William S. Smith, NOVEMBER 13, 1787

Let us dare to read, think, speak and write.

—**John Adams,** A Dissertation on the
Canon and the Feudal Law, 1765

Those who expect to reap the blessings of freedom must, like men, undergo the fatigue of supporting it.

—Thomas Paine, The American Crisis, No. 4, SEPTEMBER 12, 1777

That no man should scruple, or hesitate a moment to use arms in defense of so valuable a blessing [as freedom], on which all the good and evil of life depends, is clearly my opinion; yet arms . . . should be the last resource.

—**George Washington**, *letter to George Mason*, APRIL 5, 1769

We are not to expect to be translated from despotism to liberty in a featherbed.

—**Thomas Jefferson**, *letter to the Marquis de Lafayette*, APRIL 2, 1790

It is a common observation here (Paris) that our cause is the cause of all mankind, and that we are fighting for their liberty in defending our own.

—**Benjamin Franklin**, *letter to Samuel Cooper*, 1777

The people are the only sure reliance for the preservation of our liberty.

—**Thomas Jefferson**, *letter to James Madison*, 1787

The natural progress of things is for liberty to yield and government to gain ground.

> —**Thomas Jefferson,** *letter to Colonel Edward Carrington,* MAY 27, 1788

I believe there are more instances of the abridgment of the freedom of the people by gradual and silent encroachments of those in power than by violent and sudden usurpations.

> —**James Madison,** *address at the Virginia Convention,* JUNE 16, 1788

I have sworn upon the altar of God eternal hostility against every form of tyranny over the mind of man.

> —**Thomas Jefferson,** *letter to Benjamin Rush,* SEPTEMBER 23, 1800

When people talk of the freedom of writing, speaking or thinking I cannot choose but laugh. No such thing ever existed. No such thing now exists; but I hope it will exist. But it must be hundreds of years after you and I shall write and speak no more.

> —**John Adams,** *letter to Thomas Jefferson,* JULY 15, 1818

Our liberty depends on the freedom of the press, and that cannot be limited without being lost.

—Thomas Jefferson, *letter to James Currie*, JANUARY 28, 1786

It behooves every man who values liberty of conscience for himself, to resist invasions of it in the case others.

—**Thomas Jefferson,** *letter to Benjamin Rush,* 1803

Freedom is not a gift bestowed upon us by other men, but a right that belongs to us by the laws of God and nature.

—**Benjamin Franklin,** Maxims and Morals from Dr. Franklin, 1807

Kings or parliaments could not give the rights essential to happiness . . . We claim them from a higher source—from the King of kings, and the Lord of all the earth. They are not annexed to us by parchments and seals. They are created in us by the decrees of Providence which establish the laws of our nature. They are born with us; exist with us; and cannot be taken from us by any human power without taking our lives.

—**John Dickinson,** "Of the Right to Freedom; and of Traitors," 1804

The liberty enjoyed by the People of these States of worshipping
Almighty God, agreeably to their Consciences, is not only among the
choicest of their Blessings, but also of their Rights.

—**George Washington**, *message to Quakers*, 1789

The fundamental source of all your errors, sophisms, and false
reasoning, is a total ignorance of the natural rights of mankind. Were
you once to become acquainted with these, you could never entertain
a thought, that all men are not, by nature, entitled to a parity of
privileges. You would be convinced, that natural liberty is a gift of
the beneficent Creator, to the whole human race; and that civil liberty
is founded in that; and cannot be wrested from any people, without
the most manifest violation of justice.

—**Alexander Hamilton**,
"The Farmer Refuted," 1775

The most important bill in our whole code is that for the diffusion
of knowledge among the people. No other sure foundation can be
devised, for the preservation of freedom and happiness.

—**Thomas Jefferson**, *letter to
George Wythe*, AUGUST 1786

Liberty cannot be preserved without a general knowledge among the people, who have a right . . . and a desire to know; but besides this, they have a right, an indisputable, unalienable, indefeasible, divine right to that most dreaded and envied kind of knowledge, I mean of the characters and conduct of their rulers.

—**John Adams,** A Dissertation on the
Canon and the Feudal Law, 1765

In those wretched countries where a man cannot call his tongue his own, he can scarce call anything his own. Whoever would overthrow the liberty of a nation must begin by subduing the freeness of speech; a thing terrible to publick traytors.

—**Benjamin Franklin,** Dogwood
Papers, *written by Franklin in
1722, at the age of sixteen*

EQUALITY AND JUSTICE

All men are created equal.

—**Thomas Jefferson**, *Declaration
of Independence*, JULY 4, 1776

There can be no truer principle than this—that every individual
of the community at large has an equal right to the protection of
government.

—**Alexander Hamilton**, *speech at
Constitutional Convention*, JUNE 29, 1787

Negro slavery is an evil of colossal magnitude.

—**John Adams**, *letter to Abigail Adams*, 1819

It being among my first wishes to see some plan adopted by which slavery in this country may be abolished by law.

—George Washington, *letter to John F. Mercer*, SEPTEMBER 9, 1786

All, too, will bear in mind this sacred principle, that though the will of the majority is in all cases to prevail, that will to be rightful must be reasonable; that the minority possess their equal rights, which equal law must protect, and to violate would be oppression.

—**Thomas Jefferson**, *First Inaugural Address*, MARCH 4, 1801

As mankind becomes more liberal, they will be more able to allow that those who conduct themselves as worthy members of the community are equally entitled to the protection of civil government. I hope ever to see America among the foremost nations in examples of justice and liberality.

—**George Washington**, *message to Catholics*, 1789

God who gave us life gave us liberty. And can the liberties of a nation be thought secure when we have removed their only firm basis, a conviction in the minds of the people that these liberties are of the Gift of God? That they are not to be violated but with His wrath? Indeed, I tremble for my country when I reflect that God is just; that His justice cannot sleep forever.

—**Thomas Jefferson**, *regarding the issue of slavery*, Notes on the State of Virginia, 18, 1781

Slavery is such an atrocious debasement of human nature, that its very extirpation, if not performed with solicitous care, may sometimes open a source of serious evils.

> —**Benjamin Franklin**, An Address to the Public
> from the Pennsylvania Society for Promoting
> the Abolition of Slavery, and the Relief of Free
> Negroes Unlawfully Held in Bondage, 1782

Every master of slaves is born a petty tyrant. They bring the judgement of heaven upon a country. As nations cannot be rewarded or punished in the next world, they must be in this. By an inevitable chain of causes and effects, Providence punishes national sins, by national calamities.

> —**George Mason**, *from debates of*
> *Constitutional Convention*, AUGUST 22, 1787

The turpitude, the inhumanity, the cruelty, and the infamy of the African commerce in slaves have been so impressively represented to the public by the highest powers of eloquence that nothing that I can say would increase the just odium in which it is and ought to be held. Every measure of prudence, therefore, ought to be assumed for the eventual total extirpation of slavery from the United States.

> —**John Adams**, *letter to Robert*
> *J. Evans*, JUNE 8, 1819

During the course of a long life in which I have made observations on public affairs, it has appear'd to me that almost every war between the Indians and the whites has been occasion'd by some injustice of the latter toward the former. It is indeed extremely imprudent in us to quarrel with them for their lands, as they are generally willing to sell, and sell at such good bargains: And a war with them is so mischievous to us, in unsettling frequently a great part of our frontier, and reducing the inhabitants to poverty and distress, and is besides so expensive, that it is much cheaper as well as more honest, to buy their lands than to take them by force.

—**Benjamin Franklin,** *from his autobiography*

It is emphatically the province and duty of the judicial department to say what the law is. . . . If two laws conflict with each other, the courts must decide on the operation of each. . . . This is of the very essence of judicial duty.

—**John Marshall,** *in* Marbury v. Madison, 1803

Equal and exact justice to all men . . . freedom of religion, freedom of the press, freedom of the person under the protection of the habeas corpus; and trial by juries impartially selected—these principles form the bright constellation that has gone before us.

—**Thomas Jefferson,** *First Inaugural Address,* MARCH 4, 1801

The judicial power ought to be distinct from both the legislative and executive, and independent upon both, that so it may be a check upon both, as both should be checks upon that.

—**John Adams**, Thoughts on Government, 1776

Facts are stubborn things; and whatever may be our wishes, our inclinations, or the dictates of our passions, they cannot alter the state of facts and evidence.

—**John Adams**, *from his defense of the British soldiers in the Boston Massacre Trials*, DECEMBER 1770

It is better to toss up cross and pile [heads or tails] in a cause than to refer it to a judge whose mind is warped by any motive whatever, in that particular case. But the common sense of twelve honest men gives still a better chance of just decision than the hazard of cross and pile.

—**Thomas Jefferson**, Notes on the State of Virginia, 1785

Justice is indiscriminately due to all, without regard to numbers, wealth, or rank.

—**John Jay**, *in* Georgia v. Brailsford, 1794

Injustice, wrong, injury excites the Feeling of Resentment, as naturally and necessarily as Frost and Ice excite the feeling of cold, as fire excites heat, and as both excite Pain. A Man may have the Faculty of concealing his Resentment, or suppressing it, but he must and ought to feel it. Nay he ought to indulge it, to cultivate it. It is a Duty. His Person, his Property, his Liberty, his Reputation are not safe without it. He ought, for his own Security and Honour, and for the public good to punish those who injure him, unless they repent, and then he should forgive, having Satisfaction and Compensation. Revenge is unlawfull. It is the same with Communities. They ought to resent and punish.

—**John Adams**, *from his diary,* MARCH 4, 1776

RELIGION, MORALITY, AND VIRTUE

No people can be bound to acknowledge and adore the invisible hand, which conducts the Affairs of men more than the People of the United States. Every step, by which they have advanced to the character of an independent nation, seems to have been distinguished by some token of providential agency.

—George Washington, *First Inaugural Address*, APRIL 30, 1789

We are not in a world ungoverned by the laws and power of a superior agent. Our efforts are in his hand and directed by it; and he will give them their effect in his own time.

—Thomas Jefferson, *letter to David Barrow*, MAY 1, 1815

It does me no injury for my neighbor to say there are twenty Gods, or no God.

—Thomas Jefferson, Notes on the State of Virginia, 1782

There is in all Men something like a natural Principle which enclines them to Devotion or the Worship of some unseen Power.

—**Benjamin Franklin**, Articles of Belief and Acts of Religion, NOVEMBER 20, 1728

No Man has a more perfect Reliance on the alwise, and powerful dispensations of the Supreme Being than I have nor thinks his aid more necessary.

—**George Washington**, *letter to William Gordon*, MAY 13, 1776

Had the doctrines of Jesus been preached always as purely as they came from his lips, the whole civilised world would now have been Christian.

—**Thomas Jefferson**, *letter to Benjamin Waterhouse*, JUNE 26, 1822

Any system of religion that has anything in it that shocks the mind of a child, cannot be a true system.

—**Thomas Paine**, The Age of Reason, 1794–1795

I never told my own religion, nor scrutinized that of another. I never attempted to make a convert, nor wished to change another's creed. I have ever judged of the religion of others by their lives. . . . For it is in our lives, and not from our words, that our religion must be read.

—**Thomas Jefferson,** *letter to Margaret Bayard Smith,* AUGUST 6, 1816

I have examined all religions, as well as my narrow sphere, my straightened means, and my busy life, would allow; and the result is that the Bible is the best Book in the world. It contains more philosophy than all the libraries I have seen.

—**John Adams,** *letter to Thomas Jefferson,* DECEMBER 25, 1813

I believe in one God and no more, and I hope for happiness beyond this life. I believe in the equality of man; and I believe that religious duties consist in doing justice, loving mercy, and endeavoring to make our fellow creatures happy.

—**Thomas Paine,** The Age of Reason, 1794–1795

I consider the doctrines of Jesus as delivered by himself to contain the outlines of the sublimest system of morality that has ever been taught but I hold in the most profound detestation and execration the corruptions of it which have been invented. . . .

—**Thomas Jefferson,** *letter to*
Henry Fry, JUNE 17, 1804

No man complains of his neighbor for ill management of his affairs, for an error in sowing his land, or marrying his daughter, for consuming his substance in taverns . . . in all these he has liberty; but if he does not frequent the church, or then conform in ceremonies, there is an immediate uproar.

—**Thomas Jefferson,** Notes on
the State of Virginia, 1782

Statesmen, my dear Sir, may plan and speculate for liberty, but it is Religion and Morality alone, which can establish the Principles upon which Freedom can securely stand. The only foundation of a free Constitution is pure Virtue, and if this cannot be inspired into our People in a greater Measure, than they have it now, they may change their Rulers and the forms of Government, but they will not obtain a lasting liberty.

—**John Adams,** *letter to*
Zabdiel Adams, JUNE 21, 1776

We are firmly convinced . . . that with nations, as with individuals, our interests soundly calculated, will ever be found inseparable from our moral duties.

—**Thomas Jefferson**, *Second Inaugural Address*, MARCH 4, 1805

Contrary habits must be broken, and good ones acquired and established, before we can have any dependence on a steady, uniform rectitude of conduct.

—**Benjamin Franklin**, Maxims and Morals from Dr. Franklin, 1807

Government has no Right to hurt a hair of the head of an Atheist for his Opinions. Let him have a care of his Practices.

—**John Adams**, *letter to John Quincy Adams*, JUNE 16, 1816

Have you ever found in history, one single example of a nation, thoroughly corrupted, that was afterwards restored to virtue? And without virtue there can be no political liberty.

—**John Adams**, *letter to Thomas Jefferson*, DECEMBER 21, 1819

No point of Faith is so plain, as that Morality is our Duty; for all Sides agree in that. A virtuous Heretick shall be saved before a wicked Christian.

—Benjamin Franklin, Dialogue between Two Presbyterians, APRIL 10, 1735

Virtue alone is sufficient to make a man great, glorious and happy.

—**Benjamin Franklin,**
Maxims and Morals from Dr. Franklin, 1807

My father convinced me that nothing was useful which was
not honest.

—**Benjamin Franklin,**
Maxims and Morals from Dr. Franklin, 1807

He who permits himself to tell a lie once, finds it much easier to do
it a second and third time, till at length it becomes habitual; he tells
lies without attending to it, and truths without the world's believing
him. This falsehood of the tongue leads to that of the heart, and in
time depraves all its good dispositions.

—**Thomas Jefferson,** *letter to
Peter Carr,* AUGUST 19, 1785

Let no pleasure tempt thee, no profit allure thee, no ambition corrupt
thee, no example sway thee, no persuasion move thee to do anything
which thou knowest to be evil; so thou shalt live jollily, for a good
conscience is a continual Christmas.

—**Benjamin Franklin,**
Maxims and Morals from Dr. Franklin, 1807

Here is my Creed. I believe in one God, the Creator of the Universe. That He governs it by His Providence. That He ought to be worshipped. That the most acceptable service we render to Him is in doing good to His other Children. That the soul of Man is immortal, and will be treated with Justice in another Life respecting its conduct in this. These I take to be the fundamental points in all sound Religion, and I regard them as you do in whatever Sect I meet with them. As to Jesus of Nazareth, my Opinion of whom you particularly desire, I think the System of Morals and his Religion, as he left them to us, is the best the World ever saw, or is likely to see.

—**Benjamin Franklin**, *letter to Ezra Stiles*, MARCH 9, 1790

PEACE, WAR, AND
THE MILITARY

If there must be trouble let it be in my day, that my child may
have peace.

—**Thomas Paine**, The American
Crisis, No. 1, DECEMBER 19, 1776

To discerning men, nothing can be more evident, than that a peace
on the principles of dependence, however limited . . . would be to the
last degree dishonorable and ruinous.

—**George Washington**, *letter to
John Banister*, APRIL 21, 1778

I rejoiced at the return of peace. We are now friends with England and with all mankind. I hope it will be lasting, and that mankind will at length, as they call themselves reasonable creatures, have reason and sense enough to settle their differences without cutting throats. May we never see another war! For in my opinion there never was a good war or a bad peace.

> —**Benjamin Franklin,** *letter to Josiah Quincy III,* SEPTEMBER 11, 1783

I have never known a peace made, even the most advantageous, that was not censured as inadequate, and the makers condemned as injudicious or corrupt. "Blessed are the peacemakers" is, I suppose, to be understood in the other world; for in this they are frequently cursed.

> —**Benjamin Franklin,** *letter to John Adams,* OCTOBER 12, 1781

Peace and friendship with all mankind is our wisest policy, and I wish we may be permitted to pursue it.

> —**Thomas Jefferson,** *letter to Charles William Frederic Dumas,* MAY 6, 1786

There is nothing so likely to produce peace as to be well prepared to meet an enemy.

—George Washington, *letter to Elbridge Gerry*, JANUARY 29, 1780

But by the all-powerful dispensations of Providence, I have been protected beyond all human probability or expectation; for I had four bullets through my coat, and two horses shot under me, yet escaped unhurt, although death was leveling my companions on every side of me!

—**George Washington**, *letter to his brother John A. Washington, describing the Battle at the Monongahela during the French and Indian War,* JULY 1755

I love peace, and I am anxious that we should give the world still another useful lesson, by showing to them other modes of punishing injuries than by war, which is as much a punishment to the punisher as to the sufferer.

—**Thomas Jefferson**, *letter to Tench Coxe,* MAY 1, 1794

So strong is this propensity of mankind to fall into mutual animosities, that where no substantial occasion presents itself, the most frivolous and fanciful distinctions have been sufficient to kindle their unfriendly passions and excite their most violent conflicts.

—**James Madison**, The Federalist Papers, No. 10, NOVEMBER 23, 1787

War involves in its progress such a train of unforeseen and unsupposed circumstances . . . that no human wisdom can calculate the end. It has but one thing certain, and that is to increase taxes.

—**Thomas Paine,** Prospects
on the Rubicon, 1787

Peace with all the world is my sincere wish. I am sure it is our true policy, and am persuaded it is the ardent desire of the government.

—**George Washington,** *letter to Rev.
Jonathan Boucher,* AUGUST 15, 1798

A navy is our natural and only defense.

—**John Adams,** *letter to Congress,* 1780

It is the object only of war that makes it honorable. And if there was ever a just war since the world began, it is this in which America is now engaged.

—**Thomas Paine,** The American
Crisis, No. 5, MARCH 21, 1778

Men may speculate as they will; they may talk of patriotism; they may draw a few examples from ancient story, of great achievements performed by its influence; but whoever builds upon it as a sufficient Basis for conducting a long and [bloody] War will find themselves deceived in the end. . . . A great and lasting War can never be supported on this principle alone. It must be aided by a prospect of Interest or some reward. For a time, it may of itself push Men to Action, to bear much, to encounter difficulties; but it will not endure unassisted by Interest.

—**George Washington**, *letter to*
John Banister, APRIL 21, 1778

In times of peace the people look most to their representatives; but in war, to the executive solely.

—**Thomas Jefferson**, *letter to Caesar*
A. Rodney, FEBRUARY 10, 1810

My first wish is to see this plague to mankind banished from off the Earth, and the sons and daughters of this world employed in more pleasing and innocent amusements than in preparing implements and exercising them for the destruction of mankind.

—**George Washington**, *letter to*
David Humphreys, JULY 25, 1785

Be it remembered, then, that there are tumults, seditions, popular commotions, insurrections, and civil wars, upon just occasions as well as unjust.

> —**John Adams**, Novanglus Papers, 1774

Whensoever hostile aggressions . . . require a resort to war, we must meet our duty and convince the world that we are just friends and brave enemies.

> —**Thomas Jefferson**, *letter to Andrew Jackson*, DECEMBER 3, 1806

Discipline is the soul of an army. It makes small numbers formidable; procures success to the weak, and esteem to all.

> —**George Washington**, *"Letter of Instructions to the Captains of the Virginia Regiments,"* JULY 29, 1759

The only way to form an army to be confided in, was a systematic discipline, by which means all men may be made heroes.

> —**John Adams**, *quoted in Ralph Waldo Emerson's journal*, AUGUST 1851

I have seen enough of one war never to wish
to see another.

—Thomas Jefferson, *letter to
John Adams*, APRIL 25, 1794

Every citizen [should] be a soldier. This was the case with the Greeks and the Romans, and must be that of every free state.

—**Thomas Jefferson**, *letter to James Monroe*, 1813

For a people who are free, and who mean to remain so, a well-organized and armed militia is their best security.

—**Thomas Jefferson**, *message to Congress*, NOVEMBER 8, 1808

To place any dependence upon militia, is, assuredly, resting upon a broken staff.

—**George Washington**, *letter to the president of Congress*, SEPTEMBER 24, 1776

Without a decisive naval force we can do nothing definitive. And with it, everything honorable and glorious.

—**George Washington**, *letter to Marquis de Lafayette*, NOVEMBER 15, 1781

Perhaps no country ever experienced more sudden and remarkable advantages from any measure of policy than we have derived from the arming for our maritime protections and defense.

—**John Adams**, *State of the Union Address*, DECEMBER 8, 1798

The national defense must be provided for as well as the support of Government; but both should be accomplished as much as possible by immediate taxes, and as little as possible by loans.

—**John Adams**, *State of the Union Address*, NOVEMBER 12, 1797

Overgrown military establishments are under any form of government inauspicious to liberty, and are to be regarded as particularly hostile to republican liberty.

—**George Washington**, *Farewell Address*, SEPTEMBER 17, 1796

The spirit of this country is totally adverse to a large military force.

—**Thomas Jefferson**, *letter to Chandler Price*, FEBRUARY 28, 1807

POLITICS AND PATRIOTISM

Politics are such a torment that I would advise every one that I love not to mix with them.

> —**Thomas Jefferson**, *letter to Martha Jefferson Randolph*, FEBRUARY 11, 1800

I agree with you that in politics the middle way is none at all.

> —**John Adams**, *letter to Horatio Gates*, MARCH 23, 1776

Politics, like religion, hold up the torches of martyrdom to the reformers of error.

> —**Thomas Jefferson**, *letter to James Ogilvie*, AUGUST 4, 1811

No sooner has one Party discovered or invented an Amelioration of the Condition of Man or the order of Society, than the opposite Party belies it, misconstrues it, misrepresents it, ridicules it, insults it, and persecutes it.

—**John Adams,** *letter to Thomas Jefferson,* JULY 9, 1813

If I could not go to heaven but with a party, I would not go there at all.

—**Thomas Jefferson,** *letter to Francis Hopkinson,* MARCH 13, 1789

[The spirit of party] serves always to distract the public councils and enfeeble the public administration. It agitates the community with ill-founded jealousies and false alarms; kindles the animosity of one part against another; foments occasionally riot and insurrection.

—**George Washington,** *Farewell Address,* SEPTEMBER 17, 1796

Gentlemen, you will permit me to put on my spectacles, for, I have grown not only gray, but almost blind in the service of my country.

—**George Washington,** *searching for his glasses before delivering the Newburgh Address,* MARCH 15, 1783

My country has in its wisdom contrived for me the most insignificant office [the vice-presidency] that ever the invention of man contrived or his imagination conceived.

—John Adams, *letter to Abigail Adams*, DECEMBER 19, 1793

Men by their constitutions are naturally divided into two parties: 1. Those who fear and distrust the people, and wish to draw all powers from them into the hands of the higher classes. 2. Those who identify themselves with the people, have confidence in them, cherish and consider them as the most honest and safe, although not the most wise depository of the public interests. In every country these two parties exist; and in every one where they are free to think, speak, and write, they will declare themselves.

—**Thomas Jefferson,** *letter to Henry Lee*, AUGUST 10, 1824

Men often oppose a thing merely because they have had no agency in planning it, or because it may have been planned by those whom they dislike.

—**Alexander Hamilton,** The Federalist Papers, No. 70, 1788

If the present Congress errs in too much talking, how can it be otherwise in a body to which the people send 150 lawyers, whose trade it is to question everything, yield nothing, and talk by the hour? That 150 lawyers should do business together ought not to be expected.

—**Thomas Jefferson,** *from his autobiography*

When a man assumes a public trust, he should consider himself as public property.

> —**Thomas Jefferson**, *remark to Baron Alexander von Humboldt, from Ayner,* Life of Thomas Jefferson, 1834

If a due participation of office is a matter of right, how are vacancies to be obtained? Those by death are few; by resignation none.

> —**Thomas Jefferson**, *letter to E. Shipman*, JULY 12, 1801

I have heard of some great man, whose rule it was, with regard to offices, never to ask for them, and never to refuse them; to which I have always added, in my own practice, never to resign them.

> —**Benjamin Franklin**, *letter to Mrs. Jane Mecom*, MARCH 1, 1766

Whenever a man has cast a longing eye on offices, a rottenness begins in his conduct.

> —**Thomas Jefferson**, *letter to Tench Coxe*, 1799

My affections were first for my own country,

and then, generally, for all mankind.

—Thomas Jefferson, *letter to
Thomas Law*, JANUARY 15, 1811

Guard against the impostures of pretended patriotism.

—**George Washington**, *Farewell Address*, SEPTEMBER 17, 1796

The patriot, like the Christian, must learn that to bear revilings & persecutions is a part of his duty; and in proportion as the trial is severe, firmness under it becomes more requisite & praiseworthy.

—**Thomas Jefferson**, *letter to James Sullivan*, MAY 21, 1805

It is in the man of piety and inward principle, that we may expect to find the uncorrupted patriot, the useful citizen, and the invincible soldier. God grant that in America true religion and civil liberty may be inseparable and that the unjust attempts to destroy the one, may in the issue tend to the support and establishment of both.

—**John Witherspoon**, *from his sermon*, MAY 17, 1776

Our obligations to our country never cease but with our lives.

—**John Adams**, *letter to Benjamin Rush*, APRIL 18, 1808

Be a listener only, keep within yourself, and endeavor to establish with yourself the habit of silence, especially on politics. In the fevered state of our country, no good can ever result from any attempt to set one of these fiery zealots to rights, either in fact or principle. They are determined as to the facts they will believe, and the opinions on which they will act. Get by them, therefore, as you would by an angry bull; it is not for a man of sense to dispute the road with such an animal.

—**Thomas Jefferson**, *letter to his grandson, Thomas Jefferson Randolph*, NOVEMBER 24, 1808

Citizens, by birth or choice, of a common country, that country has a right to concentrate your affections. The name of American, which belongs to you in your national capacity, must always exalt the just pride of patriotism more than any appellation derived from local discriminations.

—**George Washington**, *Farewell Address*, SEPTEMBER 17, 1796

FAMILY AND FRIENDS

Is there no way for two friendly souls to converse together, although the bodies are 400 miles off. Yes, by letter. But I want a better communication. I want to hear you think, or to see your thoughts.

—**John Adams,** *letter to Abigail Adams*
from the Continental Congress, 1776

It gives me more pleasure than I can express, to learn that you sustain with so much fortitude the shocks and terrors of the times. You are really brave, my dear. You are a heroine, and you have reason to be. For the worst that can happen can do you no harm. A soul as pure, as benevolent, as virtuous and pious as yours, has nothing to fear, but everything to hope and expect from the last of human evils.

—**John Adams,** *letter to Abigail*
Adams, JULY 7, 1775, *referring to the Battle*
of Bunker Hill that Abigail watched with
John Quincy from a hill near their home

She prov'd a good and faithful helpmate, assisted me by attending the shop; we throve together, and have ever mutual endeavour'd to make each other happy. . . .

—**Benjamin Franklin** *about his wife,*
Deborah, from his autobiography

Where there's marriage without love, there will be love without marriage.

—**Benjamin Franklin,**
Poor Richard's Almanack, MAY 1734

Keep your eyes open before marriage, half shut afterwards.

—**Benjamin Franklin,** Maxims and
Morals from Dr. Franklin, 1807

The married state is, after all our jokes, the happiest, being comfortable to our natures. Man and woman have each of them qualities and tempers in which the other is deficient, and which in union contribute to the common felicity. Single and separate they are not the compleat human being; they are like the odd halves of scissors; they cannot answer the end of their formation.

—**Benjamin Franklin,** *letter to*
a young man, JUNE 25, 1745

My enthusiasm for Sports and Inattention to Books, allarmed my Father, and he frequently entered into conversation with me upon the Subject. I told him [I did not] love Books and wished he would lay aside the thoughts of sending me to Colledge. What would you do Child? Be a Farmer. A Farmer? Well I will shew you what it is to be a Farmer. You shall go with me to Penny ferry tomorrow morning and help me get Thatch. I shall be very glad to go Sir. Accordingly next morning he took me with him, and with great good humour kept me all day with him at Work. At night at home he said Well John are you satisfied with being a Farmer. Though the Labour had been very hard and very muddy I answered I like it very well Sir. Ay but I don't like it so well: so you shall go to School to day. I went but was not so happy as at the Creek Thatch.

—**John Adams**, Diary and Autobiography
of John Adams, 1755–1780

John has Genius and so has Charles. Take care that they don't go astray. Cultivate their Minds, inspire their little Hearts, raise their Wishes. Fix their Attention upon great and glorious Objects, root out every little Thing, weed out every Meanness, make them great and manly. Teach them to scorn Injustice, Ingratitude, Cowardice, and Falsehood. Let them revere nothing but Religion, Morality, and Liberty.

—**John Adams**, *letter to Abigail
Adams*, APRIL 15, 1776

I rather wish that he might lead a life of as little indulgence and dissipation as should be thought necessary to relax and keep his spirits. . . . [He is to be] restrained from the practice of those follies and vices which youth and inexperience but too naturally lead into.

—**George Washington**, *letter to Rev. Jonathan Boucher, 1768, about the schooling of his stepson, Jacky Custis*

Teach your child to hold his tongue, he'll learn fast enough to speak.

—**Benjamin Franklin**, Poor Richard's Almanack, 1734

At my Father's table he liked to have, as often as he could, some sensible friend or neighbor to converse with, and always took care to start some ingenious or useful topic for discourse, which might tend to improve the minds of his children. By this means he turned our attention to what was good, just, and prudent in the conduct of life; and little or no notice was ever taken of what related to the victuals on the table, whether it was well or ill dressed, in or out of season, of good or bad flavor, preferable or inferior to this or that other thing of the kind, so that I was bro't up in such a perfect inattention to these matters as to be quite indifferent to what kind of food was set before me, and so unobservant of it that to this day if I am asked I can scarcely tell a few hours after dinner what I dined upon.

—**Benjamin Franklin**, *from his autobiography*

A Brother may not be a Friend, but a Friend will always be a Brother.

—Benjamin Franklin, Poor Richard's Almanack, MAY 1752

As much as I converse with sages and heroes, they have very little of my love and admiration. I long for rural and domestic scene, for the warbling of birds and the prattling of my children.

—**John Adams**, *letter to Abigail Adams*, MARCH 16, 1777

The happiest moments of my life have been the few which I have passed at home in the bosom of my family.

—**Thomas Jefferson**, *letter to Francis Willis, Jr.*, APRIL 18, 1790

'Tis true, the regard and friendship I met with from persons of worth, and the conversation of ingenious men, gave me no small pleasure; but at that time of life, domestic comforts afforded the most solid satisfaction, and my uneasiness at being absent from my family, and longing desire to be with them, made me often sigh in the midst of cheerful company.

—**Benjamin Franklin**, *recalling a trip to London in 1757, from his autobiography*

He is a delightful little fellow. I love him too much.

—**John Adams**, *letter to Abigail Adams writing about Charles*, 1780

I must study politics and war, that my sons may have the liberty to study mathematics and philosophy, geography, natural history, and naval architecture, navigation, commerce, and agriculture, in order to give their children a right to study painting, poetry, music, architecture, statuary, tapestry and porcelain.

—**John Adams,** *letter to Abigail Adams,* MAY 12, 1780

All who saw my grandson Benny agreed of his being an uncommonly fine boy, which brought often afresh to my mind the idea of my son Franky, tho' dead many years ago, whom I have seldom since seen equal'd in every thing, and whom to this day I cannot think of without a sigh.

—**Benjamin Franklin,** *from his autobiography*

Should you or Lawrence therefore behave in such a manner as to occasion any complaint being made to me, you may depend upon losing that place which you now have in my affections and any future hopes you may have from me. But if, on the contrary, your conduct is such as to merit my regard, you may always depend upon the warmest attachment and sincere affection of your friend and uncle.

—**George Washington,** *letter to his nephew George Steptoe Washington as Washington prepared to leave Mount Vernon to assume the presidency,* 1788

I cannot afford to give gold watches to children. When you are more of a man, perhaps, if you have behaved well, I may give you one, or something that is better. You should remember that I am at a great expense for your education, to pay for your board and clothing and instruction in learning that may be useful to you when you are grown up, and you should not tease me for expensive things that can be of little service to you.

—**Benjamin Franklin,** *letter to his grandson Benny Bache,* JANUARY 25, 1782

Now, sir, for my griefs! The dear partner of my life for 54 years as a wife and for many more as a lover, now lies in extremis, forbidden to speak or to be spoken to . . . If human life is a bubble, no matter how soon it breaks, if it is, as I firmly believe, an immortal existence, we ought patiently to wait the instructions of the great Teacher.

—**John Adams,** *letter to Thomas Jefferson,* OCTOBER 7, 1818

You are a member of Parliament, and one of that majority which has doomed my country to destruction. You have begun to burn our towns, and murder our people. Look upon your hands! They are stained with the blood of your relations! You and I were long friends: You are now my enemy, and I am yours.

—**Benjamin Franklin,** *letter to William Strahan, written* JULY 5, 1775, *but never sent*

No better relation than a prudent and faithful Friend.

—**Benjamin Franklin,**
Poor Richard's Almanack, MAY 1737

A slender acquaintance with the world must convince every man that actions, not words, are the true [criteria] of the attachment of his friends.

—**George Washington,** *letter to John Sullivan,* DECEMBER 15, 1779

Tranquility is the old man's milk. I go to enjoy it in a few days, and to exchange the roar and tumult of bulls and bears for the prattle of my grandchildren and senile rest.

—**Thomas Jefferson,** *letter to Edward Rutledge,* JUNE 24, 1797

You and I ought not to die before we have explained ourselves to each other.

—**John Adams,** *letter to Thomas Jefferson,* JULY 15, 1813

Be courteous to all, but intimate with few; and let those few be well tried before you give them your confidence. True friendship is a plant of slow growth, and must undergo and withstand the shocks of adversity before it is entitled to the appellation.

—George Washington, *letter to his nephew Bushrod Washington,* JANUARY 15, 1783

I see no comfort in outliving one's friends, and remaining a mere monument of the times which are past.

—**Thomas Jefferson,** *letter to Charles Pinckney,* SEPTEMBER 3, 1816

People who live long drink of the cup of life to the very bottom and must expect to meet with some of the usual dregs; and when I reflect on the number of terrible maladies human nature is subject to, I think myself favour'd in having only three incurable ones that have fallen to my share, viz., the gout, the stone, and old age, and that these have not yet deprived me of my natural cheerfulness, my delight in books and enjoyment of social conversation. There are many sorrows in this life, but we must not blame Providence inconsiderately, for there are many more pleasures. This is why I love life.

—**Benjamin Franklin,** *from his autobiography*

WISDOM OF THE FOUNDING FATHERS

Early to Bed, and early to rise,
Makes a Man healthy, wealthy, and wise.

—**Benjamin Franklin**,
Poor Richard's Almanack, 1758

Vain man! Mind your own business! Do no wrong! Do all the good
you can! Eat your canvasback ducks! Drink your Burgundy! Sleep
your siesta, when necessary, and trust in God.

—**John Adams**, *letter to Thomas
Jefferson*, MARCH 14, 1820

A Decalogue of Canons
for observation in practical life

Never put off till tomorrow what you can
do today.

Never trouble another for what you can
do yourself.

Never spend your money before you have it.

Never buy what you do not want, because it is
cheap; it will be dear to you.

Pride costs us more than hunger, thirst,
and cold.

We never repent of having eaten too little.

Nothing is troublesome that we do willingly.

How much pain have cost us the evils which
have never happened.

Take things always by their smooth handle.

When angry, count ten, before you speak;
if very angry, a hundred.

—**Thomas Jefferson**, *letter to Thomas
Jefferson Smith*, FEBRUARY 21, 1825

Associate yourself with men of good quality if you esteem your own reputation; for 'tis better to be alone than in bad company.

—George Washington, *"Rules of Civility,"* 1747

Your affectionate mother requests that I would address to you, as a namesake, something which might have a favorable influence on the course of the life you have to run. Few words are necessary with good dispositions on your part. Adore God. Reverence and cherish your parents. Love your neighbor as yourself; and your country more than life. Be just. Be true. Murmur not at the ways of providence and the life into which you have entered will be a passage to one of eternal and ineffable bliss. And if to the dead it is permitted to care for the things of this world, every action of your life will be under my regard.

—Thomas Jefferson, *letter to Thomas Jefferson Grotjan*, JANUARY 10, 1824

I could say a thousand things to you, if I had leisure. I could dwell on the importance of piety and religion, of industry and frugality, of prudence, economy, regularity and even Government, all of which are essential to the well being of a family. But I have not time. I cannot however help repeating piety, because I think it indispensable. Religion in a family is at once its brightest ornament and its best security.

—Samuel Adams, *addressing his future son-in-law, Thomas Wells*, NOVEMBER 22, 1780

The rewards . . . in this life are esteem and admiration of others—the punishments are neglect and contempt. . . . The desire of the esteem of others is as real a want of nature as hunger—and the neglect and contempt of the world as severe a pain as the gout or stone.

—**John Adams,** Discourses on Davila, 1790

Be studious in your profession, and you will be learned. Be industrious and frugal, and you will be rich. Be sober and temperate, and you will be healthy. Be in general virtuous, and you will be happy. At least, you will, by such conduct, stand the best chance for such consequences.

—**Benjamin Franklin,** *letter to John Alleyne*, AUGUST 9, 1768

An honest man can feel no pleasure in the exercise of power over his fellow citizens.

—**Thomas Jefferson,** *letter to John Melish*, JANUARY 13, 1813

To lengthen thy life, lessen thy meals.

—**Benjamin Franklin,** Poor Richard's Almanack, OCTOBER 1733

Power always thinks it has a great soul and vast views beyond the comprehension of the weak; and that it is doing God's service, when it is violating all His laws.

—**John Adams**, *letter to Thomas Jefferson*, FEBRUARY 2, 1816

A thing moderately good is not so good as it ought to be. Moderation in temper is always a virtue; but moderation in principle is always a vice.

—**Thomas Paine**, The Rights of Man, 1791

Delay is preferable to error.

—**Thomas Jefferson**, *letter to George Washington*, MAY 16, 1792

It is while we are young that the habit of industry is formed. If not then, it never is afterwards. The fortune of our lives, therefore, depends on employing well the short period of youth.

—**Thomas Jefferson**, *letter to Martha Jefferson Randolph*, MARCH 28, 1787

Give about two [hours], every day, to exercise; for health must not be sacrificed to learning. A strong body makes the mind strong.

—**Thomas Jefferson**, *letter to Peter Carr*, AUGUST 19, 1785

In general mankind, since the improvement of cookery, eat about twice as much as nature requires. Suppers are not bad if we have not din'd, but restless nights naturally follow hearty suppers after full dinners. Indeed, as there is a difference in constitutions, some rest well after those meals: it costs them only a frightful dream and an apoplexy, after which they sleep till doomsday. Nothing is more common in the newspapers than instances of people, who after eating a hearty supper, are found dead in a bed in the morning.

—**Benjamin Franklin**, *from his autobiography*

Time is money.

—**Benjamin Franklin**, *advice to a young tradesman*, 1748

If you would know the value of money, go and try to borrow some.

—**Benjamin Franklin**, Poor Richard's Almanack, 1758

Youth is the seed time of good habits, as well in nations as in individuals.

—Thomas Paine, Common Sense, 1776

Beware of little expenses.

—**Benjamin Franklin,**
Maxims and Morals from Dr. Franklin, 1807

Laziness travels so slowly that poverty soon overtakes him.

—**Benjamin Franklin,**
The Way to Wealth, JULY 7, 1757

Dost thou love life? Then do not squander time, for that's the stuff life is made of.

—**Benjamin Franklin,**
Poor Richard's Almanack, 1746

Tomorrow, every Fault is to be amended; but that Tomorrow never comes.

—**Benjamin Franklin,**
Poor Richard's Almanack, JULY 1756

The sovereign invigorator of the body is exercise, and of all exercises, walking is best.

—**Thomas Jefferson,** *letter to Thomas
Mann Randolph, Jr.,* AUGUST 27, 1786

Use no hurtful deceit; think innocently and justly and, if you speak, speak accordingly.

—**Benjamin Franklin,** *from his autobiography*

Don't throw stones at your neighbors if your own windows are glass.

—**Benjamin Franklin,**
Poor Richard's Almanack, 1736

It is better to offer no excuse than a bad one.

—**George Washington,** *letter to his niece*
Harriet Washington, OCTOBER 30, 1791

Think of three Things: whence you came, where you are going, and to whom you must account.

—**Benjamin Franklin,**
Poor Richard's Almanack, 1755

ABOUT THE
FOUNDING FATHERS

John Adams (1735–1826)—Born to a long line of yeomen farmers, Adams was a teacher, farmer, and lawyer by trade. He was driven into the Revolutionary movement by the Stamp Act and soon found himself consumed with the cause of the patriots. Adams was a member of the Continental Congress (1774–1778) and was a key figure in getting George Washington's appointment for commander and chief of the Continental Army. He was later commissioner to France and minister to Netherlands and England. He was one of the negotiators of the Treaty of Paris, the first vice president, and the second president of the United States. He died at the age of 91, on the same day as Thomas Jefferson, July 4, 1826, fifty years after the adoption of the Declaration of Independence.

Samuel Adams (1722–1803)—Born to a prosperous father who was a prominent brewer and landowner, Adams drifted from one job to another in his younger years but found his calling as an expert instigator and organizer of propaganda and Colonial resistance during the

Revolutionary period. He was a member of the Continental Congress (1774–1775), though overshadowed by his second cousin John Adams. He was later elected to lieutenant governor, interim governor, and governor of Massachusetts.

Charles Carroll (1737–1832)—Born to a wealthy landowning Irish-Catholic family in Maryland, Carroll was educated at home and abroad but was barred from public life for nearly a decade because of his Roman Catholic faith. In the 1770s he became a champion for the Revolutionary cause through his newspaper writings, and became a prominent player in the movement from then on. He was a member of the Continental Congress (1776–1778) and the only Roman Catholic to sign the Declaration of Independence. He later served as one of Maryland's first United States senators. Living to the age of 95, he became the last surviving signer of the Declaration of Independence.

John Dickinson (1732–1808)—Born to a moderately wealthy family in Maryland, Dickinson went on to study law and became involved with the Revolutionary movement with the Stamp Act. He is known as the *Penman of the Revolution* for his influential work entitled *Letters from a Farmer in Pennsylvania,* in which he refuted Great Britain's right to taxation of the colonies. He was a militia officer during the Revolutionary War; and a member of the Continental Congress (1774–1776). He did not vote in favor of the Declaration of Independence in 1776, though he supported the cause of independence during the War and thereafter.

Benjamin Franklin (1706–1790)—Born to a candle- and soap-maker, Franklin received some formal education but was largely self-taught. After an apprenticeship with his father, he went on to work as a printer with his half-brother and later founded a Colonial newspaper. He went on to publish *Poor Richard's Almanack,* which was wildly popular in the

Colonies and abroad. For a period of years, Franklin lived in England as an agent of several of the Colonies, and defended the Colonial position in the House of Commons during the Stamp Act crisis. Upon his return from Europe in 1775, he became a member of the Continental Congress (1775), and was on the committee that drafted the Declaration of Independence. He returned to Europe as a diplomat and was instrumental in garnering French aid and military assistance during the war. He negotiated the Treaty of Paris, along with John Jay and John Adams, and he played a pivotal role in the proceedings of the Constitutional Convention in May 1787. He died in 1790 at the age of 84.

Nathan Hale (1755–1776)—Hale was a Connecticut-born schoolteacher who joined the Connecticut militia and later became an officer in the Continental Army. He volunteered for an espionage mission, was caught by the British in Manhattan, and was hanged following the battle of Long Island, in 1776.

Alexander Hamilton (1757–1804)—Born in the British West Indian island of Nevis, Hamilton was schooled in the Colonies and went on to become an officer in the Continental Army, as well as aide-de-camp and staff lawyer to Washington, and later was appointed to lieutenant colonel. He was a member of the Continental Congress (1782, 1783, 1787, 1788). Not only was he an organizer of the Constitutional Convention, but was also known as the "Ratifier of the Constitution," as he was instrumental in getting the Constitution ratified by the states. He authored fifty-one of the eighty-five *Federalist Papers,* which were enormously influential in achieving ratification of the Constitution. He was the first secretary of the Treasury and founded the Bank of New York, and the *New York Post.* Hamilton was killed in a duel with Aaron Burr in 1804.

Patrick Henry (1736–1799)—Born into the Virginia gentry, Henry was a planter, businessman, and lawyer before he became involved in the Revolutionary movement. He was commander in chief of the Virginia Militia, a member of the Continental Congress (1774–1776), a member of the Virginia General Assembly and House of Burgesses, and a five-time Governor of Virginia. He is best-remembered for his fiery oratory.

John Jay (1745–1829)—Born to a wealthy merchant family in New York City, Jay was tutored privately and later studied law at King's College, the forerunner to Columbia University. He was a member of the Continental Congress (1774 to 1777, 1778, 1779) and was a key figure in achieving ratification of the Constitution with his contribution to the *Federalist Papers*. He was the governor of New York, one of the negotiators of the Treaty of Paris, and appointed by George Washington as the first chief justice of the Supreme Court.

Thomas Jefferson (1743–1826)—Born to a prominent Virginia family, Jefferson was schooled with private tutors before going to college at William & Mary and later studying law. He was a member of the Virgina House of Burgesses, member of the Continental Congress (1775, 1776, 1783–1785), and primary drafter of the Declaration of Independence. He went on to become the governor of Virginia; commissioner to France; minister to France; secretary of state, vice president, and third president of the United States. In his final years, Jefferson founded the University of Virginia. Jefferson died at the age of 83 only hours before the death of John Adams, on July 4, 1826, the fiftieth anniversary of the adoption of the Declaration of Independence.

John Paul Jones (1747–1792)—At age 12, the Scottish-born Jones became a British marine who eventually settled in Virginia. He fought for the Colonies in the American navy at the outset of the Revolutionary War. He was the first man assigned the rank of first lieutenant in the Continental Navy and is known as the "Father of the American Navy." His record of naval victories earned him the Gold Medal by Congress in 1787.

Henry Lee III (1756–1818)—Born in Virginia and educated at the forerunner to Princeton University, Lee put a legal career on hold to enter the Revolutionary War. Known as "Light-horse Harry," he was an unsurpassed cavalry commander during the War, a member of the Virginia Legislature, member of the Continental Congress (1785–1788), governor of Virginia, and a member of the United States House of Representatives. He was also the father of Robert E. Lee.

James Madison (1751–1836)—Born to prosperous Virginia plantation owners, Madison was the eldest of twelve children. He attended what would become Princeton University and was the first post-graduate student at the school. He was a member of the Virginia legislature; member of the Continental Congress (1780–1783), delegate to the Constitutional Convention; United States congressman, secretary of State, and fourth President of the United States. He is known as the "Father of the Constitution," and was the chief architect of the document. He authored twenty-nine of *The Federalist Papers,* which played a pivotal role in achieving ratification of the Constitution. As a member of the first U.S. Congress, he sponsored the Bill of Rights. As secretary of State, he engineered the Louisiana Purchase of 1803. And as president, he successfully led the country through the War of 1812.

John Marshall (1755–1835)—Born in a log cabin in rural Virginia, the eldest of fifteen children, Marshall was largely educated by private tutors. He was a captain in the Revolutionary War and served with George Washington at Valley Forge. He was a member of the Virginia House of Burgesses, minister to France, a United States congressman, secretary of State, and chief justice of the Supreme Court, a position that he held for 34 years. While Chief Justice, he had an enormous impact on the judicial system, established the doctrine of judicial review, and participated in more than one thousand legal decisions.

George Mason (1725–1792)—Born to a family of wealthy Virginia plantation owners, Mason was brought up largely by an uncle after his father died when he was 10. He became one of the richest men in Virginia, owning thousands of acres in Virginia and in and around Ohio. He was a member of the Virginia House of Burgesses, author of the Virginia Constitution and Virginia Bill of Rights, delegate to the Constitutional Convention but failed to sign the Constitution out of criticism that it failed to effectively protect citizens' rights. He is considered the "Father of the Bill of Rights," as he was the principal author of and an advocate for the document.

John Peter Gabriel Muhlenberg (1746–1807)—Son of Henry Melchior Muhlenberg, a founder of the Lutheran Church in America, the younger Muhlenberg became a pastor himself and was a member of the Virginia House of Burgesses. In 1775, he famously finished his sermon and left to join Washington's troops. He served throughout the war and was promoted to major general. He later served as both a United States congressman and senator.

Thomas Paine (1737–1809)—Born in rural England, Paine worked as a corset-maker, inventor, and pamphleteer before emigrating to America at the age of 37 on the advice of Benjamin Franklin. His pamphlet series entitled "The American Crisis" and signed "Common Sense" was highly influential in furthering the cause for American independence. He served in the Continental Army and continued to write installments of "The Crisis" devoted to the Revolutionary cause. He later went back to Europe where he wrote *The Rights of Man* in defense of the revolutionary movement in France. After being banned from England for treason and imprisoned and nearly executed in Paris as an Englishman, Paine returned to America at the invitation of President Thomas Jefferson but lived his remaining years in poverty and isolation.

John Parker (1729–1775)—Massachusetts-born farmer and soldier from the French and Indian War, Parker commanded his militia at the Battle of Lexington on April 19, 1775. He was ill with consumption and was unable to participate in any future battles. He died five months later.

William Prescott (1726–1795)—Massachusetts-born American Colonel during the Revolutionary War, Prescott fortified Breed's Hill on the night of June 16, 1775, and commanded his troops the next day in the Battle of Bunker Hill. To conserve ammunition, Prescott famously told his troops, "Don't one of you fire 'til you see the whites of their eyes."

Josiah Quincy III (1744–1775)—A Massachusetts-born lawyer and patriot, Quincy wrote many articles in support of the cause for freedom, most notably his work called "Observations of the Act of Parliament Commonly Called the Boston Port Bill with Thoughts on Civil Society and Standing Arms." In 1774 he was sent on a secret mission to England to advocate the cause of the Colonists to sympathetic British politicians but died at sea from tuberculosis on his return trip.

Benjamin Rush (1745–1813)—Born near Philadelphia to a family of farmers, his father died when Rush was five, and he was brought up by a maternal uncle who provided for his schooling. He graduated from what is now Princeton University, studied medicine in Philadelphia, and earned his medical degree from the University of Edinburgh. He was a member of the Continental Congress (1776, 1777), a signer of the Declaration of Independence, surgeon general of the Continental Army, and treasurer of the United States Mint. He set up the first free medical clinic and later helped to found the first American anti-slavery society.

George Washington (1732–1799)—The first son of Augustine Washington and his second wife, Mary, the younger Washington was educated largely at home by his father and elder half-brother, Lawrence. He was eleven when his father died then lived with his mother at Ferry Farm in Fredericksburg, Virginia, and visited his brother at Mount Vernon, which he inherited upon Lawrence's death. He obtained his surveying license from the College of William & Mary in 1749. In 1754, he was commissioned as a lieutenant colonel and fought in the French and Indian War from 1755 to 1758, whereupon he retired to Mount Vernon to live the life of a gentleman farmer. In 1759, he married Martha Parke Custis, a wealthy widow with two children. He was a member of the Virginia House of Burgesses and a member of the Continental Congress (1774, 1775); elected to command all Continental armies in June 1775; and led successful campaign against the British forcing their surrender on October 19, 1781. He again retired to Mount Vernon, but resumed his public duties when he was unanimously chosen as the first president under the new Constitution. He was unanimously reelected in 1793 but refused a third term. After a farewell address to the American people, he retired from public life. He died at the age of 67 from a severe throat infection on the night of December 14, 1799.

John Witherspoon (1723–1794)—Witherspoon was a Scottish-born clergyman who emigrated to the Colonies to accept the presidency at the College of New Jersey (forerunner to Princeton University). Advocating resistance to the Crown in his sermons, essays, and addresses, he became involved in the Revolutionary movement and was a member of the Continental Congress (1776–1779, 1780–1781, 1782) and a signer of the Declaration of Independence, and he spent the latter part of his life rebuilding the college that had been burned and destroyed in part by the British during the War.